CASTLES AND MANSIONS

Alan James

Wayland

Houses and Homes

Building Homes
Castles and Mansions
Homes in Cold Places
Homes in Hot Places
Homes in Space
Homes in the Future
Homes on Water
Mobile Homes

All words printed in
bold are explained in
the glossary on page 30

*The author wishes to dedicate this book to
Eric Claussen*

Cover illustration: Leeds Castle, in Kent, England,
was built as a fortified manor house, and later
became a royal palace.

Editor: Sarah Doughty
Designer: Sally Boothroyd

First published in 1988 by
Wayland (Publishers) Ltd.,
61 Western Road, Hove,
East Sussex BN3 1JD, England

© 1988 Wayland (Publishers) Ltd

Typeset by Direct Image Photosetting, East Sussex
Printed in Italy by G. Canale & C.S.p.A., Turin
Bound in Belgium by Casterman S.A., Tournai

British Library Cataloguing in Publication Data
James, Alan
Castle and Mansions – (Houses and Homes).
1. Castles – Great Britain – Juvenile literature.
2. Country Homes – Great Britain – Juvenile
literature.
I. Title.
941.
ISBN 1-85210-197-0

Contents

Fortified buildings   4

Wooden castles   6

Stone castles   8

Attack   10

Defence   12

Concentric castles   14

Building a castle   16

Castles as homes   18

Castles around the world   20

Other famous castles   22

Palaces   24

From manor houses to mansions   26

Mansions   28

Glossary   30

Books to read   31

Index   32

Fortified buildings

Throughout history, people of all **civilizations** have needed homes where they could protect themselves against their enemies. Strong defences or **fortifications** were built to provide protection against attack.

A castle was a home built by a king or nobleman who had conquered a new land and needed to prevent his enemies from winning it back. A castle was a fortress, built in such a way as to provide protection for the owner, his family and possessions.

The word 'castle' usually means the fortifications built after the Normans invaded Britain in 1066, but there were many built all over the world before this date. The first forts to be built were hill forts. These were built in high places so that the defenders could see enemies at a distance. It is still possible to see the remains of Maiden Castle in Dorset, a huge hill fort built in the Iron Age.

The Romans learned a great deal by examining the remains of old fortifications and developed their own building skills when they took over Europe. The Romans built forts throughout their vast Empire to station their troops. Early forts were built of wood, but were later replaced using stone. Large Roman forts were made up of many buildings surrounded by thick walls, gates and **turrets**.

Right *The remains of Maiden Castle, Dorset in Britain. It was a huge hill fort built in the late Iron Age. The large ditches that surround the area provided defence against attack.*

Inside, a fort could hold hundreds of soldiers. In the centre was the army headquarters, with rooms to store weapons and a strongroom for money. A fort included a chapel where the **regimental standard** was kept, a bakehouse, a bath house and large barracks where soldiers slept. A village of **civilians** often grew up outside a fort.

The name given to a Roman fort was *castrum*, and it is from this that we get our word 'castle'. However, these forts were not strictly castles. A castle was the private fortress of a ruler which served as his or her home and the base from where he or she defended the land.

Above The Great Wall of China is a fortification built several thousand years ago. When completed, it stretched some 2,400 km in length.

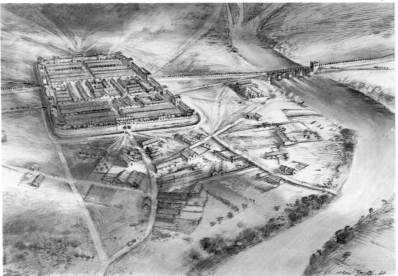

Left The Romans built many forts similar to this for their soldiers throughout Europe.

5

Wooden castles

The earliest castles were called **motte** and **bailey** castles and were built in Britain after the Norman Conquest in the eleventh century. William the Conqueror and his **barons** from France knew a great deal about the **military** use of castles as they had fought to defeat enemies in their own country.

Early castles consisted of a small fort (or **keep**) built on a small hill with a flat top called a motte. The keep was surrounded by a fence or **palisade** made up of sharp wooden stakes. At the foot of the motte was a circular courtyard, called the bailey, with a few buildings inside. The bailey of a larger castle contained a kitchen, a chapel, an **armoury**, stables, sheds, a bakehouse and a brewery for making ale. A ditch surrounded the outside of the bailey fence, which had a built-in **drawbridge** that could be raised or lowered over the ditch.

A motte and bailey castle.

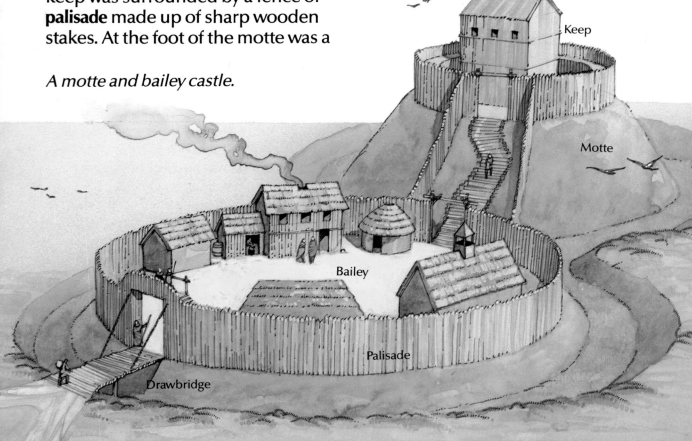

Keep

Motte

Bailey

Palisade

Drawbridge

The keep, and the buildings in the bailey were all built of wood or **wattle and daub**. The keep was built of strong timber, several storeys high. The **basement** was usually kept as the storeroom. Above this, reached by a flight of stairs, was the hall or living room. On the next floor, in the area under the roof were the **solar** or sleeping quarters. The keep on the top of the motte was the safest place to be if enemy soldiers broke into the bailey.

Above *Many wooden castles were built in Normandy in France. This shows an attack on the motte and bailey castle at Dinan, from the Bayeux Tapestry.*

Although large numbers of these castles were built, many of them were replaced by stone towers or walls in later years. These provided a greater protection against enemies than wooden castles.

7

Stone castles

Wooden castles were easily destroyed by fire, so by the middle of the twelfth century, many wooden castles began to be replaced by strong stone castles. In places where stone was readily available it was used instead of wood, otherwise stone was used to strengthen existing wooden castles.

A stone wall, called a **curtain wall,** was built around a bailey. This wall had **battlements** — regular gaps along the tops of the walls. Inside the castle wall, a stone keep was built. It was so heavy that it was usually built on flat, solid ground rather than on a motte which would be unable to support it.

Cut-away diagram of a castle keep.

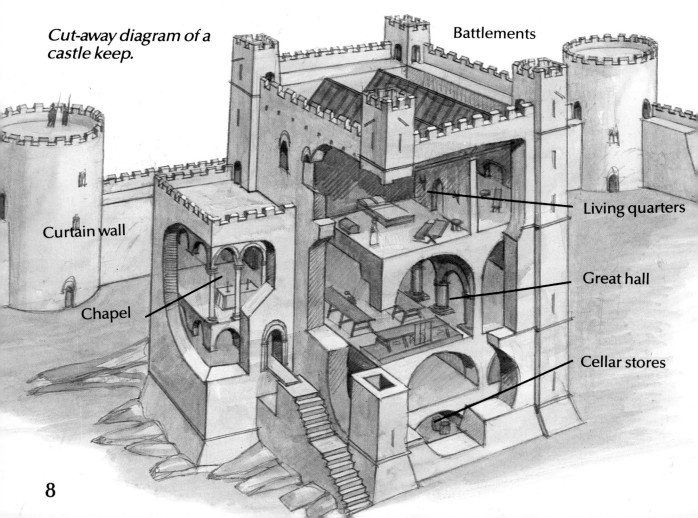

Battlements

Living quarters

Great hall

Cellar stores

Curtain wall

Chapel

__Right__ Restmorel Castle in Britain. A shell keep replaced the wooden palisade at the top of the motte. Inside the shell are stone buildings.

The castle keep was the safest place inside a castle and was where the owners lived. Above the basement storeroom, the first floor of the keep was occupied by the great hall, where the lord and lady received visitors and held banquets. In early castles the family would sleep in an alcove in the thick walls, but later the bedroom was usually the room above the hall. Most castles had a private chapel for the family, a **privy**, but no kitchen because the cooking usually took place in a building in the bailey.

Despite the solid appearance of the large, square stone keeps, they had their weaknesses, and were gradually replaced by **shell keeps**. Some of the earliest stone castles were shell keeps. This was a strong circular wall often built around the motte of an old wooden castle. The wooden castles were destroyed to make way for buildings of stone. Sometimes these keeps had round rather than square walls. This was because the corners of square keeps could be easily broken down by enemies. By the thirteenth century the circular wall and round tower had become common all over Europe.

The changing design of castles was influenced by the methods of attack and defence in warfare.

Attack

Although a castle was a home, nobody living inside could forget that it was also a fortress, designed to keep an enemy out. An attacking army was faced with a very difficult task when trying to get inside a castle.

The attackers relied on speed, surprise and skill to invade a castle.

Above The ruins of Château Gaillard, a strong fortress in France.

One method was to try to stop food and supplies from entering a castle. When the people inside ran out of stores they were forced to come out. Sometimes the enemy was able to trick someone inside a castle to open a gate or lower the drawbridge.

In the days before guns and explosives, attackers would try to scale castle walls or knock them down. There were many weapons that were used to damage a castle. Attackers might try and force their way in using a battering-ram. This was a strong tree trunk with an iron tip used by teams of men who rammed the machine against the castle gate or walls. Other machines, such as the catapult, used twisted ropes to throw heavy stones at the castle. A trebuchet or 'bouncer' was a huge catapult used to hurl heavy rocks or stones at castle walls or throw missiles over the top.

Tall ladders were used to try to climb over the castle walls. Great wooden siege towers were built and propped up against the walls. These protected the attackers from the fire of arrows from overhead.

Siege tower

Trebuchet

Battering-ram

Attacking a castle

Sometimes miners, called 'sappers', tunnelled under the corner walls of a castle. They then propped up the tunnel roof with wooden supports and set fire to it. As the wood burned, the tunnel and part of the wall fell in. This method was used as part of the attack on Château Gaillard in France, one of the most difficult castles to enter in the whole of Europe.

11

Defence

The siege of a castle could last for several weeks or months. As no food supplies could reach the castle during this time, the defenders had to fight back as hard as they could before being forced to surrender.

Many castles were well fortified against attack. By the fourteenth century most castles had a drawbridge over a ditch or moat, which could be lifted in times of attack. The entrance to the castle was blocked by a huge gate covered with sheet-iron, called a **portcullis.**

The portcullis was controlled from the **gatehouse.** The gatehouse contained winding devices to raise and lower the drawbridge and portcullis. Some castles had several portcullises at the main gate, and enemies could become trapped between them. Often there was a **murder-hole** in the ceiling above where missiles could be dropped on the heads of the attackers.

Defenders would fight from the safety of the castle towers. They fired arrows from the top of the battlement walls, or from the arrow slits at various levels in the castle walls. From this height, missiles could be dropped on the enemy below. Wooden **hoards** with slatted floors were attached to the top of castle walls for this purpose. Sometimes the defenders poured boiling liquid, or a burning substance called 'Greek Fire', on the enemy soldiers below.

Left The gatehouse of Harlech Castle, Wales, was strong enough to hold out when the rest of the castle had been overrun by the enemy.

Moat

Hoards

Portcullis

Greek Fire

*Soldiers defending a
castle from the
battlements at the top of
the castle towers.*

Usually the defenders would
surrender because they lacked
ammunition, food or manpower.
Sometimes they were worn out by
the constant attack, or by being cut
off from their supplies and **allies**.

13

Concentric castles

Castles with very strong defences were very rarely attacked. Some of the strongest castles were built with **concentric walls**. This meant the castle had two sets of walls, with the outer wall lower than the inner wall. Soldiers on the inner wall could fire over the heads of those on the outer wall. If attacking soldiers broke through the outer wall of the bailey, they were surrounded by archers. The inner wall was usually much stronger with enormous gatehouses and towers.

The concentric castle was not a new idea. From the fifth century the Byzantines had built fortifications with concentric walls. When the **Crusader** Knights fought in Palestine and Egypt, they saw castles without keeps, but with lines of very strong walls around their baileys instead. In their fight to make the Holy Land part of Europe the Crusaders built enormous concentric castles there. The ruins of Krak des Chevaliers, the most famous of the Crusader castles, can still be seen in Lebanon.

When the Crusaders returned to Europe, they brought the idea of concentric walls with them. They knew that these castles were able to withstand the surprise attack with a very small number of defenders. The Tower of London is a good example of the concentric castle. Many were built in Wales by King Edward I, including Harlech, Beaumaris and Caerphilly.

Right The concentric castle consisted of two sets of walls. The outer wall was lower than the inner wall, so allowed defenders to fire over the heads of those below.

Above *The heavily fortified castle of Krak des Chevaliers showing its concentric defences.*

Left *The Tower of London. The central keep is surrounded by two sets of fortified curtain walls.*

15

Building a castle

The site chosen to build a strong stone castle was of great importance. It had to be in a position to provide a natural defence such as on top of a high peak. It also had to be on an important route such as a road or a river. The surrounding land had to be able to supply the castle with food and water. It was also useful if there was stone available in the area. Otherwise, heavy stones would have to be carried over long distances to the site.

A large stone castle could take many years to build. Large quantities of rubble were needed for the **hard-core** for the foundations of the walls and buildings. Large quantities of stone from **quarries** and timber from forests were needed to build the castle.

The transport of these materials to the site and the castle construction had to be carefully planned, and required a huge work force. This was made up of masons, quarriers, smiths and carpenters, as well as large numbers of unskilled labourers. The person in charge was often the master-mason who supervised the work.

The stone-masons erected the shell of the building. They used cranes and hoists to lift the heavy materials to build the walls and towers. They often used a mixture of rubble and stones mixed with mortar that would set hard.

Left An early illustration of stone-masons building a castle tower. The stones are being hoisted by a pulley, while on the ground the stone-masons smooths the stones.

A smooth stone known as **ashlar** was often used for the outer surfaces of the castle and for strengthening the corners of the castle.

Other workmen made the floors and doors of the castle. The last areas to be finished were the living quarters. The furniture was made by the carpenters. This included tables, benches, stools, chests, beds and cupboards.

Above Castel Coco in Spain is a brick-built castle which was easier to build than a stone castle.

In the fifteenth century, stone castles were replaced by castles built with bricks. While brick was unable to stand up to the force of gunpowder now used in warfare, it made building quicker and cheaper, particularly in areas without building stone.

Castles as homes

A castle was a base where soldiers would defend and control the surrounding countryside, town or coastline under their **monarch** or ruler. But a castle was also a home for many people — the family who owned the castle, their friends, relations and servants.

Some castles were quite basic with few comforts, while others were more grand, with attractive furniture and wall tapestries. The castle hall was a large room with long tables where banquets could be held when entertaining important visitors. The baron and his family and guests would sit together on a table at one end of the great hall. Large numbers of cooks prepared the food in the kitchens. The kitchens were often separate from the living quarters because of the heat, smells and danger of fire. Facilities in a castle were few — water could be collected from a well, but there were no bathrooms, even in the grandest castles.

Life in a castle was very public. Most people lived, ate and slept crowded together. The castle owners had their own bedrooms, but most of the others slept crowded together in any space they could find — probably huddled near the fire rolled up in a blanket on the floor.

A castle was a busy, exciting place to live. There was always work to be done and the castle was maintained by local craftsmen. Even small castles had carpenters, saddlers, blacksmiths, armourers and shoesmiths. Larger castles would have cooks, candlemakers, launderers and tailors. A castle could also have hundreds of servants.

Life in a castle was not all hard work and the people who lived there would find time to amuse themselves. They played games such as chess or draughts, or were entertained by the court **jester** or singing **minstrels** who travelled from castle to castle and brought news of distant happenings.

Right On a special occasion the lord and lady of the castle would hold a banquet. While eating, they were often entertained by jugglers, or minstrels.

18

Castles around the world

Above The ruins of the Great Zimbabwe, in southern Africa.

Below The Red Fort at Delhi, built by the Moguls from Persia.

There are castles in many parts of the world built by ancient and modern civilizations. About 1,500 years ago the great walled city of Chichen-Itza in Mexico was built by the Mayan people. In southern Africa there are still the remains of the Great Zimbabwe, built about 800 years ago by the Shona people.

In the Holy Land there are the remains of many of the Crusader castles. The building of Krak des Chevaliers was started in the twelfth century and spread over 150 years. Not only did its steep position make it difficult to attack but it was also very heavily fortified with smooth concentric walls, which were impossible to climb. This made it difficult to capture the castle by storm. Krak des Chevaliers also had a vast storage space for food and a constant supply of fresh water so the defenders could not be forced out by starvation.

India has many beautiful castles, such as the Red Fort at Delhi, built during the Middle Ages by the Moguls from Persia. The Indian castles are surrounded by walls with powerful gates at the main entrances which are often richly decorated. They were usually built to a great height to allow elephants and their mounts to enter inside. The allies of the Moguls, the Rajputs, built the Amber Palace which overlooks Jaipur city.

Castles in Japan were built with the traditional Japanese design of smaller roofs being built on top of larger ones. Himeji Castle was built by a ruler in the fourteenth century and has since been reconstructed.

In the USA, in the nineteenth century, 'log forts' were built by the Europeans as protection from Native Americans, angry at the invasion of their territory. One of these **cavalry forts** is at Fort Laramie. Another famous fort was the Alamo, where Davy Crockett and Jim Bowie died in 1836 when they fought the Mexican army.

In the USSR, the Moscow Kremlin is a castle with attractive domes on the roof. Until the seventeenth century it was the home of the Russian Tsars. It is now the seat of the Russian Government.

Below *In the USA, log forts were built to protect traders and settlers from Native Americans. This is a painting of Fort William: one of the first log forts to be built.*

Other famous castles

There are parts of the world that are very famous for their castles. The Loire Valley in France is well-known for its châteaux. A château is a word for a building such as a castle, a palace or a country house. There are châteaux in France ranging from the medieval fortresses to the later decorative palaces.

The château at Angers is a French medieval fortress designed to withstand sudden raids and long sieges. It has seventeen towers and massive curtain walls. Some of the turrets have pointed roofs which were added to the castle later.

Turrets are also a feature of German castles. Marksberg is the best preserved of the German castles built along the River Rhine. The castles were positioned where taxes could be collected from the traders who used the river. Another famous castle is the Wartburg.

Right This castle called the Burg Pfalz is built on a small island in the River Rhine in Germany.

Spain is rich in castles, especially in the area that was called Castile. The Castel de Monte is a beautiful and famous castle with a **polygonal** plan. Outside it looks like a medieval castle, but the inside shows the influence of Arab culture with tapestries, beautiful rugs and carpets. For the first time in a castle there was also the luxury of running water for baths. It was likely that this castle was used as a hunting lodge rather than as a fortress. The Castel Coco in Spain is a castle built of brick with decorations and hanging turrets. But is also had strong corner walls and gun ports like a fortress. This castle was built to be attractive as well as heavily fortified.

Above The massive round towers of the medieval fortress at Angers in France.

Left The Alcazar in Segovia, Spain was built for a fifteenth-century king. From its high position it defended the city walls.

Palaces

A palace is the official home of a ruler, such as a king or queen, prince, emperor, or an elected leader such as a president.

Many palaces were built when it was no longer necessary for rulers to live in castles for safety, but some were built much earlier. The Palace of Knossos on the island of Crete was built 4,000 years ago.

Château Azay-le-Rideau in France is a perfect example of a palace built in the style of a castle. The château has towers, turrets and a moat. But there is nothing military about it — its features are for show. The purpose of the moat is to give a reflection of the château in its waters. There are big windows to let in the light and wide staircases.

Above Chateau Azay-le-Rideau in France is a palace built in the style of a castle.

Left The famous Hall of Mirrors in Versailles in France has mirrored wall that reflects sunlight from the opposite window.

Another 'fairy tale' palace is Neuschwanstein in Bavaria, built by 'mad' Ludwig II in the nineteenth century but never completed.

The Royal Pavilion is a splendid palace at Brighton in England. This was the seaside home of King George IV, built with oriental-style domes on the roof while the inside was decorated with Chinese furnishings.

The building of royal palaces was at its height in the eighteenth century. Palaces were the centre of court life, full of courtiers and servants. King Louis XIV built a magnificent palace at Versailles, near Paris, to heighten his own importance as a ruler. It was also large enough to house all the nobles of his kingdom so he could keep them under control. With its gardens and parklands Versailles was one of the most beautiful palaces in Europe and the standard the others were judged by.

Some palaces were built with a simpler design — the Escorial near Madrid and the Winter Palace in Leningrad, Russia.

Some palaces are still used as homes for royalty or a ruler. Buckingham Palace is still the official home of Queen Elizabeth II. It contains rooms used for royal functions, the Queen's private quarters, as well as offices for her staff. The White House in Washington DC serves as the official residence of the US President. As the home of a ruler it is a palace in all but name.

Left As the official home of the President of the USA, the White House in Washington can be called a palace.

From manor houses to mansions

During the fourteenth century, large manor houses began to be built. These were fortified houses rather than large fortresses. Manor houses were usually built by wealthy merchants who felt the need to protect themselves, their families and possessions in unsettled times.

Most manor houses were built of stone and wood, and a few were

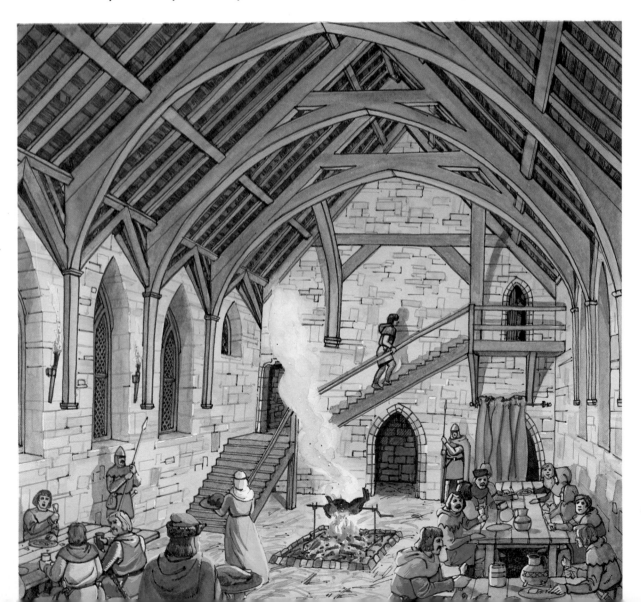

built of brick. Their roofs were tiled and their windows fitted with wooden shutters. Although manor houses had been built for hundreds of years it was the first time a single room or hall had given way to a house with several storeys. Other rooms were added such as a kitchen, a chapel and bedrooms.

Barons preferred the comfort of their manor houses, which were smaller and more comfortable than a large, draughty castle. But like castles, manor houses were designed for protection. Many were built like small castles without the high walls. They were usually fortified with strong doors, thick walls and sometimes a moat. Fortified manor houses were often given the name of castles, such as Stokesay Castle in Shropshire, and Leeds Castle in Kent, England. The stone walls of Penshurst Castle had battlements like a medieval castle. Many large manor houses copied this style.

By the sixteenth century the manor house became a mansion. Changing methods of warfare meant that battles took place in the field rather than around a castle. This meant that houses built like fortresses were no longer needed. The houses of this period had smaller, cosier rooms and very large windows to make the rooms lighter. Attractive building designs and beautiful furniture made these houses very pleasant places to live.

Left *Feasting inside the great hall at Stokesay Castle, a fortified manor house in Shropshire in Britain.*

Right *The style of a manor house often included some features of a castle. This manor house in Kent has battlements and a moat.*

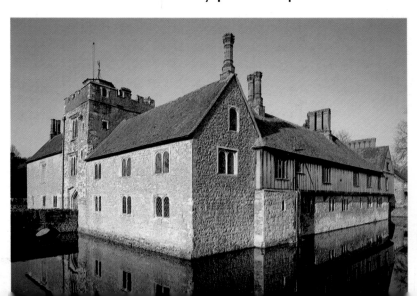

Mansions

A mansion is a large, grand home built by wealthy people, using timber, brick or stone. Mansions are beautiful buildings, designed by **architects** using the best materials and craftsmen to carry out the work.

Left San Simeon in California, USA is a mansion built in the style of a castle.

There was attention to symmetry in the building of great houses. Mansions in the USA are large, fine houses. They were often built with an attractive flight of stairs at the entrance, and pillars leading to the roof. The outside of mansions in South Carolina had **clapboard** walls, window shutters and a staircase leading to the entrance hall.

In the eighteenth century there were many grand houses built in Britain. These Georgian mansions were large country houses with magnificent rooms for entertaining guests, and large numbers of bedrooms. They also had a library, a picture gallery and a wine cellar. All the rooms would have graceful furniture and a stove for warmth. The main buildings of the mansion were joined by long corridors to the

Right A colonial mansion in Charleston, South Carolina, USA.

wings of the house where the kitchen and other rooms were situated. Life in a mansion was very comfortable with plenty of servants to manage the work in the house and gardens.

Some famous buildings that were built as castles became mansions. In the seventeenth century Kenilworth Castle was a stately mansion. Some people were still building homes in the style of castles early this century. Castle Drogo, a mansion in Devon, England was only finished in 1930. A famous fake castle in the USA is San Simeon in California, built in the 1920s by millionaire William Randolph Hurst. This was put together by using parts of buildings from all over Europe.

Mansions have replaced the castles of earlier times as grand homes built to last.

Glossary

Allies   Friendly countries or states that join together for a common purpose.

Ammunition   A supply of arrows or gunpowder for warfare.

Architect   A building designer.

Armoury   A place for storing weapons.

Ashlar   Cut stone with a smooth, straight finish.

Bailey   A courtyard with buildings, surrounded by a fence.

Baron   A member of the nobility with a titled rank.

Basement   The part of a building below ground level.

Battlements   Walls of a building with openings to fire guns or arrows.

Cavalry fort   A defended place with soldiers on horseback.

Civilizations   Groups of people with highly developed lifestyles.

Clapboard   Pieces of overlapping wood on the outside of a building.

Civilians   People not in the armed forces.

Concentric walls   Two walls, one enclosed inside the other.

Crusaders   Christians who wanted to win back the Holy Land from the Muslims in the Middle Ages.

Curtain wall   A strong wall surrounding a bailey.

Drawbridge   A bridge over a moat or ditch that can be drawn up.

Fortification   A structure that protects or defends.

Gatehouse   The fortified gateway to a castle, used for defence.

Hard-core   Stones or rubble used as a foundation for buildings.

Hoards   Platforms built out from castle walls to overhang the wall, for the purpose of throwing missiles down below.

Jester   A comedian or 'fool' at court, employed to amuse the company.

Keep   The great tower, and strongest part of a castle.

Military   To do with soldiers and warfare.

Motte   A large mound of earth on which a tower was built.

Minstrel   A medieval singer or musician.

Monarch   A ruler with a title.

Murder-holes   Holes in the roof of a passage through which defenders could drop objects on attackers.

Palisade   A strong wooden fence.

Portcullis   A metal-covered gate that could be dropped quickly to protect an entrance.

Privy   A small lavatory.

Polygonal   Many sided.

Quarry   A place where stone is obtained from the ground.

Regimental standard   The special emblem or flag for a particular group of soldiers.

Shell keep   A wall around the top of a motte.

Solar   The private quarters of the lord and lady and their family within the castle.

Turrets   Small towers on a building.

Wattle and daub   Mud or clay plastered on to a framework of woven sticks.

Books to Read

Castles by Richard Clark (Wayland, 1985).

Castles by Jenny Vaughan (Franklin Watts, 1984).

Homes by Molly Harrison (Ernest Benn, 1973).

Look at Castles by Alfred Duggan (Panther, 1960).

Explore a Castle by Brian Davison (Hamish Hamilton, 1982).

See Inside a Castle by R.J. Unstead (Hutchinson, 1977).

Buildings by Alan James (Batsford, 1975).

A History of Building Materials by Norman Davey (Phoenix House, 1961).

Houses and Homes by Theodore Rowland-Entwistle (Wayland, 1985).

The Castle Story by Sheila Sancha (Kestrel Books, 1979).

Picture Acknowledgements

The author and publishers would like to thank the following for allowing their illustrations to be reproduced in this book: Aerofilms 9; Mark Bergen 19; Sally and Richard Greenhill 5 (top); Michael Holford 7; the Hutchison Library 12, 15 (both), 20 (top); John James 6, 8, 11, 13, 14, 24, 26; Leeds Castle Foundation *cover*; National Trust Photographic Library 27; Peter Newark's Western Americana 21; Ronald Sheridan's Ancient Art and Architecture Collection 17, 20 (bottom), 22, 24 (top), 29; Topham 10, 24 (bottom); ZEFA Picture Library 23 (both), 25, 28. All other pictures from the Wayland Picture Library.

Index

Numbers in **bold** refer to
illustrations

Africa 20
Alamo 21
Alcazar **23**
Angers 22, **22**
Amber Palace 20
Azay-le-Rideau 24, **24**

banquet 9, 18, **19**
battering-ram 10, **11**
battlements 8, 12, **13**, 27
Bavaria 25
Bayeux Tapestry **7**
Beaumaris Castle 14
brick castles 17, **17**, 22
Brighton 25
Buckingham Palace 25
Burg Pfalz **23**
Byzantines 14

Caerphilly Castle 14
Castel Coco **17**, 22
Castel de Monte 22
Castle Drogo 29
cavalry forts 21
Château Gaillard **10**, 11
Chichen-Itza 20
concentric walls 14, **14**, **15**
Crusaders 14, 20
curtain wall 8, **8**, **15**, 22

Drawbridge 6, 10, 12

Egypt 14

Escorial 25

forts 4, **4**, **5**, 6
Fort William **21**
France 6, 11, 22, **22**, 25, **25**

gatehouse 12, **12**, 14
Germany 22, **23**
Great Wall of China **5**
Great Zimbabwe 20, **20**
Greek Fire 12, **13**
Gun ports 22
Gunpowder 17

Hall of Mirrors **24**
Harlech Castle **12**, 14
Himeji Castle 21
Hoards 12, **13**

India 20, **21**

Japan 21

keep 6, 7, **8**, 9, 14
Kenilworth Castle 29
kitchen 9, 18
Knossos 24
Krak des Chevaliers 14, **15**, 20
Kremlin 21

Lebanon 14
Leeds Castle 27
log forts 21, **21**

Maiden Castle 4, **4**
Marksberg 22

moat 12, 24 27
motte and bailey 6, **6**, **7**
murder-hole 12

Neuschwanstein 25
Normans 4, 6

polygonal castle 22
portcullis 12, **13**

Red Fort 20, **20**
Restmorel Castle **9**
Romans 4, 5, **5**
Royal Pavilion 25

San Simeon **28**, 29
sappers 11
shell keep 9, **9**
siege tower 10, **11**
South Carolina 28, **29**
Spain **17**, 22, **23**, 25
Stokesay Castle **26**, 27
stone-masons 16, **16**

Tower of London 14, **15**
trebuchet 10, **11**
turrets 4, 22, 24

USA 21, 25, **25**, 28, **28**, 29, **29**
USSR 21, 25

Versailles **24**, 25

Wartburg 22
White House, The 25, **25**
Winter Palace 25

LEABHARLANN CHONTAE LONGFOIRT
(Longford County council)

This book may be retained for three weeks. Afterwards fines of 5p per week or portion of a week plus any postage incurred will be charged.

The latest date entered below is the date by which the book should be returned.